Two Sisters
The story of Mary and Martha

Luke 10:40-42

"Martha, Martha," the Lord answered, "you are worried and upset about many things, but few things are needed— or indeed only one. Mary has chosen what is better, and it will not be taken away from her."

Written and
illustrated by
Janis Cox

Two Sisters: The story of Mary and Martha
Copyright © 2024 by Janis Cox

ISBN: 978-1-990870-08-8

Published by Butterfly Beacons www.janiscox.cox

Library and Archives Canada Cataloguing in Publication

Cox, Janis, 1949-
Two Sisters: The story of Mary and Martha/Janis Cox.
ISBN 978-1-990870-08-8 (print)

1. Title

This story is based on Luke 10:40-42

As Jesus and his disciples were on their way, he came to a village where a woman named Martha opened her home to him. She had a sister called Mary, who sat at the Lord's feet listening to what he said. But Martha was distracted by all the preparations that had to be made. She came to him and asked, "Lord, don't you care that my sister has left me to do the work by myself? Tell her to help me!"

"Martha, Martha," the Lord answered, "you are worried and upset about many things, but few things are needed—or indeed only one. Mary has chosen what is better, and it will not be taken away from her."

The sound of pots banging downstairs echoed through the early morning stillness.

"Where is Mary? Why is she not here to help me?" Martha muttered as she went outside to pick some grapes.

From her bed on the rooftop, Mary looked up at the sun as it appeared above the hill.

It had been a hot day. She was grateful that she and her sister had slept on the roof where it was much cooler.

She sighed as she thought about her sister who always worked - cleaning, cooking, spinning wool and grinding grain. She thought she should get out of bed and help.

Instead, thoughts about the last few days tumbled into her mind. Tonight, they were having guests and one guest was Jesus of Nazareth.

The lesson he taught a few days ago made her see everything differently. He said they should love God with all their heart, all their soul, all their mind and all their strength.

She knew she could do that. But then He said they should love everyone else the same way. That was the hard part - to love everyone.

"Mary! Get up." Martha's voice penetrated her thoughts.

Scurrying down the ladder, she missed the last step and landed almost directly at Martha's feet.

Startled, Martha wanted to say something unkind. Instead, laughter bubbled up inside her and smothered thoughts of scolding her sister. It started as a snicker.

Then she laughed out loud. Now she couldn't stop and tears rolled down her face.

Mary stared at her sister. She, too, joined in on the laughter. Martha helped Mary to her feet. She hugged her tightly.

"Oh Mary, sometimes you are too much. Get something for breakfast. Then grab a towel. We have much to do before our guests arrive."

This was an important day. Not only was Jesus coming for dinner, but he was bringing his friends.

Martha wanted everything to be perfect. She had planned a special meal, but she needed Mary's help to get it ready.

After breakfast, Martha and Mary each went about their tasks. Mary hummed a tune while she worked. Sometimes she stopped, stared off into the distance, and thought about what Jesus had said.

Martha kept busy with her own chores and didn't notice that Mary sometimes stopped working.

The day went by quickly until there wasn't much time left before Jesus would arrive. Martha searched out Mary. She saw her down on her knees, reaching inside a cabinet.

"Mary, are you finished in this room?"

Mary glanced up at Martha. She had found a jar of perfume at the back of the cabinet. She knew the perfect use for it. (1)

1 - To know Mary's plan read John 12:3-8.

Yes, I am all done," Mary said. "Should we get ourselves cleaned up for our visitors?"

Martha glanced around the room. Mary had done her jobs well. However, Martha could think of other tasks to make this event perfect.

Mary gave Martha a long, pleading look.

Maybe it would be better to get ready. They could work together on those little extras after the guests had arrived.

"Yes," Martha answered. "Let's get cleaned up. We don't want them to find us in our work clothes, do we?"

They climbed the ladder to their bedroom and helped each other get ready to meet their guests.

Off in the distance, they heard a hearty laugh.

"That's Jesus," said Mary.

Gathering up their skirts, they climbed down the ladder. Mary went slowly this time. She didn't want another tumble like this morning.

They hurried out the door and walked arm-in-arm to welcome Jesus and his disciples.

Oh, it was so good to see them. They looked tired, dusty, and thirsty.

Martha shouted, "Welcome! Come in and rest yourselves."

After they sat down, Mary brought them a bowl of water and a towel to clean their feet. She made sure each guest had a pillow on which to sit and a cup of wine. Martha had already left for the kitchen.

The room went silent. Jesus started speaking. His voice drew Mary closer. She saw a spot open near his feet. She sat down and curled her legs under her.

Jesus spoke.

What he said was so real, so true, so exciting - she couldn't leave, not yet. She needed to be here. She relaxed, listened, and learned.

All worries left her. She left behind the dishes, the food and the cleaning. Mary started to see something bigger - a God who had created her, a God who loved her and had plans for her.

Martha entered the living room. "Mary, I have been looking for you. I need you to help me."

"Lord," she questioned Jesus, "isn't it important to you that my sister left me alone to complete all the work? Tell her to help me."

Mary glanced up at her sister.

She started to rise.

Jesus put his hand on her shoulder and gently guided her to sit back down.

Looking at Martha, he said, "Martha, Martha, you are worried and upset about many things. Mary has made the right choice, and no one can take it away from her."

Martha stared at Jesus.

She turned around as she struggled to keep the tears away.

As she continued toward the kitchen, she muttered, "I am not going to cry in front of all these people."

"Is Mary right, and am I wrong? I only want to do my best and have everything go the way I planned."

Who does He think He is?" she thought.

She stopped.

She knew who He was. He was the Christ, the Son of God.

Yes, that is the truth. He is the Son of God.

The memory of his words cut deeply into her soul. He knew what was important - He said Mary was doing what was right.

Should she go into the other room and listen to Jesus? Did she, the perfect planner, need to learn at the Master's feet, too?

She had done almost everything she thought was necessary. But there was always something more. Do, do ... do.

Maybe taking time with Him is more important than always doing?

What does God want of me?
She stopped and listened.

Voices carried from the other room.

His voice, calm, confident, and solid. The disciples' voices were soft, questioning. Her heart stirred. She turned. Jesus said Mary was doing what was better.

Would it be better for her, too?

"I need to..." she murmured.

"You need me," she heard in the stillness.

"What will they think if everything is not perfect?" she whispered to the heavens.

She heard these words from the Scriptures: "It is God who arms me with strength and makes my way perfect." (2)
God is perfect. I need God.
2 - Read 2 Samuel 22:23 to find this scripture.

Slowly, she stepped away from her preparations and towards her Lord.

Activities

1. **Build a house:**

Make a house for Mary and Martha to live in. Use shoeboxes or cardboard. Remember to put furniture on the roof, too.

2. **Make dough:**

Create some dough (refer to the dough recipe in this book - it hardens after baking and you can paint it) for dolls, furniture, pots and pans, etc. Paint your creations. Then put them in the house. Act out the story.

3. **Make a play:**

Use this story to make a play to show to your friends or family. You could use puppets, too. You can find a few ways to make puppets in this book.

4. **Draw pictures:**

Draw your own pictures to go with this story. Then "read" your story through the pictures.

5. **Research:**

Research New Testament times - housing, food, clothing and people. Decide what you want to learn. Check out books in the library or online. Use this information and put it together in a book form. Give your book a title.

6. **Story writing:**

Create your own stories based on other people in the Bible. Read about a person in the Bible. For instance, read about Noah, Moses, or Daniel. Then rewrite the story in your own words.

7. **Plan a party:**

Decide whom to invite. Decide what food and drinks to serve. Decide on a time of arrival and departure.

Don't make the planning of the party take over from your enjoyment when your guests arrive.
Make sure you take time to enjoy your guests.
Relax and have fun at your party.

8. **Questions:**

Is there a friend who sometimes makes you upset? How do you handle this situation?

Consider what Jesus said about loving everyone. How can you apply that to your life?

Are you so busy that you don't have time to dream, pray, or listen to God?

Do you often prefer your own way and resist listening to others? This is a common experience. Take a moment to actively listen to those around you. Recall a time when you felt frustrated because things didn't go as planned. Think about how you could respond differently the next time it happens.

Salt Dough Recipe

To make people, furniture, and other creations for your house, you can use this salt dough recipe. You can bake the creations in the oven to harden them or let them air dry, which might take two or three days.

Ingredients:
- 2 cups flour
- 1 cup salt
- 2 tablespoons cooking oil
- Up to 1 cup water

Directions:
1. Put the flour in a bowl. Mix in the salt.
2. Add the oil and then gradually add the water while stirring.
3. Once the mixture starts to come together, use your fingers to mix it. If needed, wet your fingers with additional water and continue mixing.
4. Knead the dough on a cutting board until it is smooth and rubbery, which may take about 10 minutes.
5. Form your figures. If you need to make joints, ensure they are well stuck together by using a little water.

Baking Instructions:
1. Preheat the oven to 250°F.
2. Place your creations on a foil-lined cookie sheet.
3. Bake for one hour.
4. Remove from the oven and let cool. For thorough drying, bake again for the same amount of time after they have cooled. Note: Larger pieces may require more time to dry completely.

Air Drying Option:
- You can also leave your creations out to dry on the counter, but this might take two or three days.

Finishing:
- Once your creations are completely dry and cool, paint them with either watercolours or acrylic paints.
- Finally, spray them with a clear coat of acrylic sealer.

Puppet-Making

1. Sock Puppet
- Choose a long sock that goes up to your child's elbow. Light colours work best so the features will stand out.
- Decorate the sock using buttons or googly eyes, felt scraps, construction paper, craft foam, or other materials.
- Assemble by sewing or using glue.

2. Finger Puppet
- Take an old glove and cut off one of the fingers.
- Decorate with materials similar to those used for the sock puppet.

3. Stick Puppet
- Use a stick (tongue depressors, paint stir sticks, or popsicle sticks work well).
- Create your figure with markers, craft foam, or construction paper.

4. Paper Bag Puppet
- Decorate a paper bag with the features of your character.
- The fold of the bag can sometimes be used as a mouth.

5. Paper Plate Puppet

- Decorate the paper plate as a face using wool, markers, googly eyes, etc.
- Glue the paper plate to a paint stick for handling.

Parental References

Weaver, Joanna. *Having a Mary Heart in a Martha World.* WaterBrook Press: 2007
Weaver, Joanna.

Having a Mary Spirit. WaterBrook Press: 2006

The Bible

The story is based on these verses:

Luke 10:40-42

Author Bio

In 2001, Janis experienced a life-changing moment when she gave her life to Christ. She is an active member of two prestigious cross-Canada Christian writers' groups, The Word Guild and Inscribe.

Inspired by Joanna Weaver's book, *Having a Mary Heart in a Martha World*, Janis combined her talents as a writer and artist to create *Two Sisters*.

Janis is a retired teacher and businesswoman who has published numerous devotionals and articles. She is also the author-illustrator of two beloved children's books, *Tadeo Turtle* and *The Kingdom of Thrim*.

Her artistic journey began in 1995 when she started studying watercolour at The Haliburton School of the Arts, in Ontario, Canada.

Janis has been happily married for over 50 years and is the proud mother of three grown children and grandmother to seven wonderful grandchildren.

One of her greatest joys is sharing with others the incredible things God has done in her life.

All of Janis's books are available on Amazon. You can find them by typing "Janis Cox books" in the search bar. For more information, visit her website at www.janiscox.com

Reviews help other readers discover my books (and keep me writing) so consider leaving an honest review on Goodreads or your favourite review site. Thanks so much.

Blessings,
Janis

www.ingramcontent.com/pod-product-compliance
Lightning Source LLC
LaVergne TN
LVHW072100070426

835508LV00002B/200